A JOURNEY TO

FINANCIAL FREEDOM

A guide to flipping houses

Financial Freedom Just Ahead

STEVE RICHARDSON

A Journey to Financial Freedom

A guide to flipping houses

By: Steve Richardson

Dedication

I would like to dedicate this book to my wife and children who are my reason to always keep pursuing the next level. Without my wife, who is my best friend and without her none of this would be possible. I thank God for sending her to me to love and care for. I thank God for providing the wisdom, gifting me with information which has enabled me to become a better manager for his Glory.

I would also like to thank my spiritual fathers who have gone before me and business mentors alike who have seen the path that I was taking and been able to speak to that successful man in me.

Thank you to every investor and fund manager who believed in me and trusted me with their hard earned funds. We will continue making money together.

Table of Contents

Foreword

It was a typical day in my Beverly Hills offices 10 years ago. A handsome and well dressed young gentleman came to meet with me. His name was Steve Richardson. Someone had suggested that we meet. Today we have no recollection of who that was. We know that our meeting was far from chance.

I knew there was something very untypical about Steve Richardson. As we began to communicate with each other I was impressed with Steve's knowledge of real estate, especially at such a young age. I felt as though I was sitting with someone that was much older than his years.

It was suggested that I meet Steve to discuss re-financing 47 high-end residential properties that I owned in the Beverly Hills and Palm Springs areas. Steve's ability to articulate put me at immediate ease with him. Here we were, Steve 6 feet 7 inches tall and quiet soft-spoken. I was taken with Steve's balance between his heartwarming personality and the respectful manner in which he carried himself. Steve demands respect for himself and others.

This meeting began many years of conversation and real estate deals. At the time I was primarily involved in development and high-end residential rentals. Steve is a great researcher and magnet for resources which includes people. We have had many intense meetings with so many people that maybe we only met once. Steve has a curious and inquisitive mind that is uniquely welcoming.

Any of us as entrepreneurs in the real estate industry have our stories to tell about the down-turn of the real estate market that took place in the mid-2000's. Steve and I both have one. Unfortunately, our stories caused us to lose touch for a few years. Once, again not by chance we were brought together once again. This time we remember the person and are very grateful for the renewal of our relationship. Today we are partnering in many fix and flip deals.

I am thrilled with the content of this book that Steve has written. Steve's story truly is a gallant "Journey to Financial Freedom". Steve has masterfully shared the intimate details of his real estate career followed by the nuts and bolts of how to succeed in real estate. I have read so many books on how to fix and flip houses. They all give information on how to rehab the property. However, many fail to explain how to get into the deal.

Many people are interested in getting into real estate.

Many people are already involved in real estate. One thing many in these groups have in common is a lack of knowledge as to how to obtain alternative ways to finance a property. Sometimes financing a property with conventional hard money makes a good deal not a deal at all because of exorbitant loan costs. Many have lost all of their money in projects because of this and vow to never be involved in another rehab project. Steve is a genius at structuring alternative financing methods.

As I read this book I was blown away with the knowledge that

Steve is sharing with us all in his book. It is invaluable. It doesn't matter if you are just starting out or have many years of experience. Everyone will learn and gain financial freedom from this read if you choose to follow Steve's examples.

I have been a real estate entrepreneur for over 35 years. I continue to grow and learn from Steve's intellect and knowledge. HE has taken the mystery out of real estate investing to help make sound and secure decisions in this fascinating and challenging world.

I am grateful to have re-connected with Steve. Today, I am happily living in the Palm Springs area and focusing on the abundant choices of fix and flip properties. Although, we call it "Steve's car days" (which I know he would prefer not to have) we have many rehab projects underway. Just to keep the score even we also do rehabs in the Los Angeles area so I can have those "car days" as well.

Give yourself the best gift you could ever give yourself and your family. Read and re-read this book. We can never have enough education. Education is knowledge and the most valuable component we have to be successful as real estate investors.

There is a concept that I have always followed and truly believe, "We must give it away in order to keep it". Steve Richardson definitely lives within that concept.

Refer to this book as your real estate guide to success and you will achieve financial freedom beyond your wildest dreams.

Denise Saluto

CEO, Formulas for Success in Real Estate

Preface

My intention is that the information in this book will enlighten your mind, enliven your desire and inspire you to pursue your dream of entrepreneurship. As a society, we often learn by seeing the success and failure of another person. I have lived on both sides of the statement above and have learned some guiding principles which have helped to propel my current business to the level that it is now.

Entrepreneurs are different by design, always thinking of ways to provide a service or make a statement in their world perspective. I hope that the information and principles in this publication would light the flame in your heart to begin to move forward into your dreams and take control of things that affect your quality of life.

Work should not completely dominate our time, in life, there has to be time for reflection and play as well.

I believe that entrepreneurship is a means to that end. If we can work now in order to be able to work less in the future, we are creating financial freedom for ourselves and a financially sustainable future for our families. When we discover the truth about money and begin to build financial systems that bring in capital 24 hours a day, then we have developed a way to live free trading our time for dollars.

Introduction

By reading this book you will learn how to flip your first house, by raising the money through wholesale deals and closing the purchase with private money.

The purpose of the book is to train and inspire new investors to learn how to buy homes with what they have; little or no money down, creative financing methods, and using responsible leverage.

Chapter One

Drummer to Financier

Financial freedom is just around the corner!

This can be your journey to financial freedom.

I was born and raised in Long Beach, Ca. I was blessed to be gifted in school. I was the nerd, the misfit, the smart one who stood out. I was picked on by others throughout my school-age years.

I decided in high school that I didn't want to be a nerd anymore.

I just wanted to be normal, normal. You know that word that represents the old concept of what we believe an ideal American is.

The old adage is to go to university, have a family and work in a career for 30 years. My Father worked for the Aerospace Industry for many and years and Retired from the VA. My Mom was a civil service worker, who then became an Entrepreneur and now works managing a social services agency. They were able to provide a good life for my siblings and I, however, Neither of them achieved financial freedom from having to wake up and go to work. I view having freedom financially when you don't have to go to work anymore if you choose not to and your financial system is still paying you. Most of the citizens of America lose money every second instead of gaining money every second. Our liabilities outpace our investments and when we sleep we have bills that are accruing to the point that we have to go to work somewhere to pay those bills.

But what if you could create a financial system that pays you every minute, more than what you are charged every minute. Then you would no longer be trading your time in order to pay for your life, but the system that you created even years ago, pays you for life.

Being Free financially is to have a financial system that pays you more than enough to live for your entire life.

So back to talking about Normal.

I learned that if I dumb down maybe I had a chance of being accepted by the people that I wanted to be my peers, the jocks, the cool guys that seemed to be able to get the girls.

The more I tried the more I learned that there is nothing normal about exceptional. There was something in me that was just different, I couldn't explain it at the time of discovery but on this journey to financial freedom, I learned that there are resident gifts, special qualities that dwelled within my heart.

Your gifts are your innate qualities.

You have to learn to appreciate, accept and embrace your gifts.

Your gifts will cause doors to open for you and bring you in contact with great people in this life.

Gifts, are the things that you are naturally good at. Some people are great at sales, others excellent at administration, but I really believe that gifts are unique to each individual. Activation of your gift will eventually catapult you to greater places in life. You simply have to recognize, embrace and cultivate your gift.

 Let your gifts blossom and watch prosperity manifest in your life.

Oh and about Gifts,

My Late Uncle Big James would always tell me to stop hiding your gift. That Man; bless his soul; made a huge impact on my life as a young man and his words have stuck with me to this day.

I learned in high school that I was pretty good at making a lot of noise with drums, so I embraced drumming as a purpose. Making music was a huge part of my life. I practiced rudiments daily, listened to my favorite bands and emulated my favorite drummers until I got to the point where my style had become an amalgamation of rock, jazz, world beat, and funk.

If I felt it, I would play it, and play it LOUD. So naturally, I thought, "well I can go around the world playing drums and that would be the perfect life for me."

Later I met up with a couple of friends and we formed a band. We also began to promote live shows at different venues in Los Angeles.

Over time we grew into a movement developed a following which spawned a Record label. I have many friends that went on to earn

Grammy awards and tour with nationally recognized bands around the world, but that did not turn out to be the course of life for me.

The Godfather

I had a Godfather who was a Pastor in Los Angeles for many years. I learned early in life that I was called to be a minister. When he was up in age, he began to lose his sight. I watched him continue to preach and teach the Gospel over the years as he eventually became 100% blind. He would say to me "I see better than I ever have in my life." He would travel all over

America flying from city to city helping different congregations to learn about faith and hope.

His Mantra was the quality of my life is getting better and better.

I had some success in promotions of live music, poetry, and jazz shows. But Around 20 I met a woman who I would marry a couple of years later and there went my dream of being a pro musician full time. I had a change in priorities. My dilemma was not that I could not find a gig and go play, but how do you do that with a wife and new child when local gigs do not pay well... So I ventured into working with the disabled. Helping people with special needs and began to utilize the psychology classes that I took in both high school and college. I became pretty good at working with people, I am a pretty big guy, 6 foot 7 and maybe 250 pounds.

The human services companies would give me their most violent and high profile cases. They figured that I could handle the violent psychotic guys better than some of the other employees could because of my stature and calm demeanor.

This was true in many senses but high stress and low pay were not a good combination for a successful lifestyle with a wife and child.

(At least in Real Estate you can make a lot of money.)

So I began to work not only one job but eventually two jobs. Then two jobs became three jobs. I worked until I got to the point that there were no more hours in a day that I could work. 24 hours shifts on the weekends for years. Yeah looking back this was definitely not the way to start a great marriage. The husband goes to work every Friday and returns on Sunday or Monday night. Then he gets up on Tuesday to go work some- where else. It is great to work long hours when you have to and that is what is available. But I learned from my friend Dr. Andy who I used to play music with, that it is more important for you to make your hours more valuable than it was to sim- ply work more hours. He had a life that is enviable today, he worked four hours for four days and made more than enough money to live and master the things he wanted to in life. In his off time, he mastered oil painting, and then mastered kung fu, and then mastered the guitar.

He would travel locally and internationally at his leisure.

He had achieved a degree of financial freedom by the age of 35.

The one thing I remember him saying to me is that he designed his life to work for him.

He went on to say he never wanted to live more than ten minutes from work and wanted to be the best at each thing He took on. Success is having time for the things you truly value.

If I could find a way to make my hours worth more, ultimately I could work fewer hours. Financial freedom has something to do with actually having freedom.

The Seed of Entrepreneurship had been planted in my heart.

I would often go and visit with my friends Mom who was an entrepreneur. I admired her, she always had a new BMW and a nice condo, never once did I hear her mention anything stressful about money.

Her stress was more like, I am not sure where to buy my next warehouse. She would often encourage me to go in business for myself, I had a lot of good ideas but did not know how to manage the process of getting started on my own.

I would vacillate between the fact of work and the dream of freedom.

The time I spent working in group homes and driving my clients to work could have been spent going on hikes and working on new business ideas, however, I had not figured it out yet, and did not know where to start.

Find someone in your circle that can give you sound business advice and encourage you to move forward with your business ideas.

Word of caution, people without business experience are typically not equipped to help you become a successful entrepreneur.

A large part of your success can easily be linked to your vital connections to other successful people.

I was working three jobs to feed my family struggling to live the American dream and she was flying to China to build factories.

Something was wrong. The musical gigs and three jobs did not allow a lifestyle of peace or tranquility, it was more like an existence which included feeling sleepy, hungry, and regularly asking if this is what life truly is.. I was always working and never getting ahead.

Most jobs only allow for you to live just over broke..

Time went on but the seed of entrepreneurship had been planted. I worked all my jobs, my wife decided to leave.. probably because I was not home much, nor was I the happiest guy when I made it home after working two or three shifts. I was trying to be a great Husband and Father, but it just didn't work out in the way that I planned. My family was torn apart by divorce, I eventually moved to the east coast for a year, and after a winter of ice and sleet, I moved back to sunny southern cal with nothing more than a Volvo station wagon, old drum set, and clothes...

Chapter Two

Boom and Bust

During a conversation with my Cousin, who had been running a Mortgage company for a few years, He encouraged me to take My skills and see what I could do in the real estate field. I had trained for a real estate license 8 years before and bought the Carlton Sheets video system and never used one of the strategies that we taught.

I found myself paralyzed by the great fear of the unknown. Commission only sales jobs were unthinkable when you have obligations and no guarantees...

So I worked a corporate job in psychology and was fired immediately after Christmas vacation.

Being fired from my last job caused me to become an entrepreneur.

Sometimes the thing that lets you go only releases you into your destiny.

This turned out to be my sign to leave the east coast. I packed up and prepared to move back to CA. With no job and no home, I learned the truth of this statement.

When you have lost everything, you have nothing left to lose.

The Place I found myself living in life could have been dangerous.. I mean people can become desperate and do crazy things like believing that there must be another way to make a living besides having a nine to five job and waiting for the company to pay your salary. I still had obligations, but no way to take care of them.

So I overcame my fear and ventured into working in the mortgage industry chasing home loans on the phone in Orange County California or should I say the mortgage mecca.

There I was 28, and starting my second career that should have been my first but somehow life had taken a detour away from Real Estate success and given Me a job to support my family at the time. So I went all in, head first. It takes a laser focus to move past the initial unknowns to learning a new trade.

I came back to California with $1,000 cash, a used Volvo, an old drum set, and my clothes. The contents of my barn apartment were in storage in PA that I left after a drawn-out divorce which caused me to rethink this thing called life and career.

When you begin to see what your true value is, you begin to approach life on your terms. People that own corporations look for people that can fill their spots in order to make a profit off of their gifting and skillset. If you are great at organizing you can become the chief of organizing your department and cap out at $120,000, while they make millions off of your efforts. They pay you $120,000 minus taxes and your take home is more like $80k. After you pay all of your expenses that you gather to maintain the lifestyle of the executive you will see quickly that that plan does not work so well. $80k is not enough to set up a family for the future. I have learned after working three jobs to have a chance to live in the neighborhood I wanted to raise my kids in, and drive a car that wouldn't stop on the freeway. My work hours can not be extended beyond 24 in a day, really 8 to 10 hours a day is more than enough. The key is to make your hour worth more. I needed to learn something that would increase the value of my hour, and give me back my life.

Becoming an investor is about freedom. With the right invest-ments you have the freedom to say I want to make this much this year, and plan it out and make it happen. You also have the freedom to say I want to develop this much passive in-come that will allow me a certain lifestyle, freedom to say goodbye to my job, goodbye to my old boss.

Investing will give you the freedom to use your gifts for the benefit of your future and set up a lasting financial legacy for your family.

It may cost you your sense of security to take the leap of suc-cess, however, nothing ventured nothing gained.

Originating Mortgage loans helped me to earn the cash need-ed to buy my first investment property.

Within a year of helping a lot of my clients buy their first hous-es and fix them up, I found a house in my neighborhood that was a great value and snatched it up. My buddy had just moved back to town and started working with the firm so we decided to fix it up as a joint venture. The condo was in move in ready condition it needed nothing, but we were able to buy it under value and used the money we earned to buy a few other properties.

Each of us brought a different skill and that little condo ended up making us a $37,000 profit each. Success!

Creating community

Every house, development, and project is a chance to bring something new to a community. Putting together a team of contractors, lenders, inspectors, and tradespeople is like building a family.

Also, my favorite deals are those that come to me from the most unexpected places.

It's in those moments that I realized how a healthy, diverse community has supported my success.

I played in a free jazz, reggae and rock band up into the time I started my career in real estate.

One of my Brazilian drummer friends saw I was now the owner of a real estate company. He had a buddy that needed to sell his house, so He came to me knowing I would be able to relate to him.

We worked together to help him get out of a tough financial situation and one of my partners ended up buying the house. We partnered up rehabbed it and sold it for profit. It feels good to know that my connections made in the art and music world were also relevant in the business. Everyone came out a winner.

The best deals are always win-win scenarios.

Being an African American man in real estate has been challenging as well as rewarding.

I am often soft-spoken which can lead to people underestimating me, but I have learned to turn that into a strength.

When I was first starting my real estate business, I had a lot of great times. The market was hot, the money was moving, and deals were plentiful. I knew with the help of God many things were happening for me.

My aim then was to empower as many people as possible to help them create a better future for their families.

I started my company to simply provide home loans over time we developed into an investment brokerage which became a house buying agency. Yet not many real estate professionals were not savvy enough to turn buying and selling real estate into an actual business. Our company had a very steady loan pipeline and grossed more than our competitors, but when I looked around at the other firms in our marketplace, we were the only one of our size that was owned, operated and managed by African Americans.

And now we flip homes.... *talk about a misconception.*

Chapter Three

The Power of Mentorship

When the Student is ready the teacher will appear.

A Buddhist proverb

I met my first mentor on an Elevator

One day as I was on the elevator going to up to the mortgage office, I met a man who was wearing a negro league commemorative jersey. He began to ask me about the baseball teams expecting that I knew something about them. Little did he know, I hadn't played baseball since I was around 9 years old, and was completely uninformed of the existence of the former negro baseball league. I thought I was smart but felt pretty silly because in my life I had no interest in investigating that part of American sports history. He was loud spoken, comfortable and about 6 foot 2 and 350 pounds. It turns out that

He was an old school loan officer who had been in the industry for over 30 years. He had run a private equity investment fund which provides loans to business owners and worked on the stock exchange controlling a billion bucks. I went to meet with him and I was given the opportunity that changed my adult life. He drove an immaculately clean 560 sec Benz and took me out to dinner and there we discussed business.

He saw something in me, I had not yet noticed.

Sometimes people see you before you can see your self. They know your potential before you can recognize and embrace that innate gifting.

The Gifts you already have

You can create opportunities that will support and highlight your gifting. Many businesses have been birthed from the place of a person working diligently in his area of gifting. In that place of work, he may happen upon an idea or business process that solves another person's problem. We get paid based on the problems that we learn to solve. Your business should involve providing a service or product that solves another person problem. If you find a solution to a continual problem you can create a system that solves it, and charge others to use your solution.

He offered for me to work with him, at a higher split than what I was earning. He would make a portion of what I generated and in return, he would teach me everything he knew about the industry. I had nothing to lose and everything to gain. The team I was working with was only there to use my skills to make money and would not teach me everything I needed to know to be successful in the full spectrum of the business. So after praying about it, I took the leap and sent some loans over to him to help ensure the success of my move.

I made the move and began to work from his office. Step by step he began to give me history lessons, processing lessons, sales strategies, He would close and I would open, and eventually, I would close and he would watch and critique.

He was hard to deal with in some ways and yet extremely

thoughtful, rough yet wise and full of knowledge. We began to talk about sports, and movies and life. I learned then that your best clients are clients for life. It wasn't about the closings, it was about the process of getting to know people and genuinely caring about them. The more people you help solve their problems, the more money you make.

This statement was completely counterintuitive to everything that I had been learning. It was like going from working for the Wolf of Wall Street to working for an old seasoned pro who was in the sunset of his career and looking to pass the mantle to someone else. I was blessed to be that other person and I am forever grateful.

There were two things that I will share here that affected my view of real estate and its potential to change lives. One was this, in the beginning of my training with the Dr. he told me this.. As I stood outside of the 15 story office building he said " step away from the wall." perplexed I said OK, and stood away from the wall puzzled by what this was all about. He went on to say " picture the building that is behind as a stack of 100 dollar bills, your job is to give the money away." The more money you give away the more you make. The lender always gets a piece of what he lends.

The cash potential in real estate is virtually unlimited, the only thing you have to do is find people to give it to and you will become fabulously wealthy.

The second was this, as we were watching a football game as loud as you can imagine in his home office. "Steve, what do you think the guy is gonna do when he gets the ball and he nears the finish line?" I said run.. he said "exactly run like hell!" he went on, "When you are getting close to closing on your next deal, what are you to do? I said work on it. " No CLOSE IT! All other businesses you are focusing on must stop, you run like hell to get it closed. nothing else matters, new origination, processing new deals, dealing with hard deals.. STOP being busy and RUN Like Hell. Close it! don't Look Back Close IT~!"

In this business you have to have tenacity, it is not for the faint of heart or people that are simply trying something new. If you do not take this business seriously it will be very difficult if not impossible to see the benefits that can be attained if you simply focus and close.

Focus and Close.

The value of a mentor is literally priceless.

A mentor can help you overcome years of learning in a condensed amount of time. Consider Him like a Sherpa that is your seasoned guide, He has traveled the terrain you seek to explore, he has seen and overcome the obstacles you are destined to encounter. He has made the mistakes that you don't have to make if you take heed to his advice. The advice and guidance of a mentor is one of the most valuable things you can have. Listen to your mentor and succeed, fight your mentor and you may waste time and lose money.

If you can't find a mentor, find a coach, someone who is actively working in the business you are starting.

4 **things to never do.**

Never believe you are smarter than your mentor.

Never trust your broker with over 6 figures of your cash.

Never buy a property without multiple exit strategies.

Never buy a property from a stripper in Vegas.. (I'll talk about that deal later.)

Victory after Defeat

Successful people maintain a positive focus in life no matter what is going on around them. They stay focused on their past successes rather than their past failures, and on the next action steps, they need to take to get them closer to the fulfillment of their goals rather than all the other distractions that life presents to them. **Jack Canfield**

I clearly remember my mentor mentioning to me to stop buying properties in 2005 and into 2006. I thought he was a little off base because here I am buying a property and creating additional income. I really liked receiving checks for 5 and 6 figures and did not want to believe that would stop because of one man's opinion of the marketplace. He would say you will be able to buy a fourplex in Huntington beach and cash flow. I would reply in my own head and sometimes verbally you must be crazy. The average price for a small apartment complex in that city was over $750,000 at the time, and with mortgage rates, you could barely generate enough income to cash flow on its gross expenses. As time marched on and banks began to go belly up to began to hear his words come back to me. He had been through three 10 year real estate cycles and had 6 times the experience I had.

Never think you are smarter than your mentor.

People that have lived through things can show you things to come because there is nothing new under the sun. They may repackage it and put a new wrapper on it, but it is the same item remade by a new manufacturer. If you consider the Egyptians had ideas for a flying machine and we finally see them as normal items in our lifetime, there is nothing new under the sun.

Be wise in your timing and have multiple exit strategies for all of your investment holdings.

In the heyday of the mortgage boom, we had a few good hits in which netted us over 6 figures. My broker at the time had developed an investment strategy which was supposedly paying over 10% a month. I had made considerable money with him and trusted him too much. After listening to his investment overview over and over again I decided to invest with him against my better judgment. The problem was he could not tell me exactly what the money was buying or how the profit would be generated but he was paying out large dividends to other investors in the pool. Again I trusted him too much and invested over 6 figures with him, he returned about 20 percent of the cash invested before going belly up. I have never recovered that principal from him. Don't trust your real estate broker with large sums unless you have security for the money, and know what it is going into. I had to learn that if the investment sounds too good, it probably is.

In the beginning of my career, I had some great gains and lost everything in the market implosion. One thing I have learned is that it is better to be conservative in both your investing and your lifestyle as a whole. I have done many of the things I have set out to do in life however did not consider the goal of long term passive cash flow. I learned to generate profits actively but did not study to invest for passive cash flow. These past two years I have begun to change the investment portfolio by owning both active flip and rental properties continually.

Mission Accomplished

I think buying my first commercial property has been my biggest triumph. I managed to put together financing for a commercial building in 2013 after the market crashed. A lot of banks scrutinized me, I was a realtor with a new investment firm. I was also engaged and got married the month after we closed on the apartment building.

Getting together the will and tenacity to come back from losing everything was one of the hardest things I have learned to do.

Overcoming failure is a real test of faith. You come to find that are different types of fear that we deal with in business. There is a fear of failure and a fear of success. When you have experienced the tremendous gains that come from a successful business and live through a season of losses, there is a real toll that your psyche takes.

You go through the steps of denial, and anger, and fear and

depression and ultimately lose hope. When you have lost hope then your mind begins to look at things from a different place, your mindset that brought you to the place of confidence which helped to fuel your success has now changed to a mindset of fear and hopelessness, I call it amnesia, you completely forget that you are still a successful person and begin to settle for things that are completely below your skill set, drift into delusions of other businesses or even leave your field of expertise all together to hopefully reinvent and live in success again, in a different iteration of life.

In my case, I was fortunate to have a mentor in success and a mentor who helped through the tough times. The help of someone who has lived it already is invaluable when you are facing a slump in business. They can give you another perspective that will help you to see the light in the dark situations that you face.

There are seasons of feasting and times of famine in business.

Market conditions, client inconsistency, lack or inefficiency of marketing or closing. There are many aspects in the business cycle that have to be developed and fine-tuned to produce consistent results in favorable conditions.

It is imperative to periodically look at your business objectively to be able to identify and work through any constraints or bottlenecks that have been developed in your business process. These bottlenecks limit your team's overall performance and ultimately affect your growth, profitability and even longevity in a competitive marketplace. The small businesses that do the best are the ones that have leaders that are not so full of their own ideas that they will not listen to the voice of their trusted team mates. A great leader in the Real Estate investment field will periodically stand back and evaluate their business to see how it can improve before it is allowed to stagnate and lose its competitive edge. I have personally come to see that I am pretty good at a few things however there are people on my team that are professionals in their own right, and they excel in areas where I am only proficient. If I am only proficient in a certain skill and do not utilize the skills of the teammates; I become a potential barrier to my team's success.

Pride can cause stagnation.

When I finally found a partner at a local fund and some creative strategies to create cash for a down payment, we were able to put together the deal. I felt proud of what I had done and owning a piece of real estate on a popular main street in the city felt like a major achievement.

I am often asked the question of if I Have made any poor investment decisions?

I'm lucky to still be in the business because I do have nightmare stories, I have made many decisions I would do differently. I wish I would have flipped more property in the beginning of my career, rather than holding on to it. When the recession hit in 2008, I had nine pieces of real estate. Located nationwide $450.000 home in DC, $300,000 in FL, $850000 in Las Vegas, $700,000 in LB, $650000 in LA, $430000 in LA, $500000 in LB, $700000 in Westminster. Using the strategies that I learned at that time I was able to a mass a portfolio of

$4.58 Million, all purchased with equities earned from real estate commissions, equity stripping at repositioning, creative deal structuring, strategic partnerships and commercial banks.

At the time of the mortgage meltdown of 2009, I needed more capital to work with and didn't understand private leverage as I do now, so refinancing property in a closed alternative and subprime credit market was virtually impossible. Finding partners and creating credit are things that I learned to do. I would go to seminars and learn new strategies and implement them. I sent out the yellow letters, and placed bandit signs, wrote small ads in the newspaper, bought internet leads, purchased a market territory advertised in the yellow pages, developed websites, before I knew it, I was on the radio paying top dollar for spots daily and not looking at the amount of money I was spending on marketing on a monthly basis.

If you were to ask what are my investing goals for the future?

I would really like to build a portfolio of multifamily apartments in a working-class rental market. The goal is to buy 50 homes per year and grow it as large as can be managed. I know an investor in Los Angeles who owns 1000 units and has had this portfolio since the early 1980's. He has remained multimillion-aire years and years over because of smart decisions and leveraging talents of others and pursuing monies that were available to him.

Chapter Four

Becoming an Investor

So you are considering becoming a real estate investor?

Do you have the time and stamina to be an active investor or Is being a passive investor a better fit for you.?

Here are a few principles to consider:

First we should Look within.

> Every great dream begins with a dreamer. Always remember, you have within you the strength, the patience, and the passion to reach for the stars to change the world.

Harriet Tubman

Know yourself first; learn to gauge your threshold for risk and your ability to see a project through to the finish line. Believe in yourself, no one has more passion than you, has more talent than you, or access to more opportunities than you do. You will learn the trade and business processes along the way. Know your market, property values and consumer demand.

Make sure that you do not allow your ego to convince you that you know more than you actually know. Assess the things that you don't yet understand.

To successfully flip houses, you need to first assess your professional and financial resources. You need to know how much money you have to invest on your own or if you need to find investors. Finding investors is an art unto itself, but knowing how much cash you have to invest first is a logical first step. After you have assessed your personal cash situation, you may want to speak with your friends or family that may have an interest in investing with you. It is also wise to seek out real estate investment clubs and hard money lenders that are working in your target area in order to expand your base of contacts and possibly partners in the future.

If you don't have the money, you can find a joint venture partner or partners to pitch in cash as well. Splitting your first house profits with other partners is a great way to start, build some momentum and get your first flip under your belt. Sure, you'll have to split profits, but it's far better to get 50% of something than 100% of nothing.

If you are weak in any one of the core areas of discipline, hire someone who can help you.

Develop a Business Plan:

To succeed in business, to reach the top, an individual must know all it is possible to know about that business.

J Paul Getty

When you say business plan to a person who has not been in business before, you may as well be speaking Greek. It is important to be able to see the who what when where why and

how of what you plan to do because that is what a clear concise business plan will convey to you and your potential team and other stakeholders in your organization like money lenders and investors.

When starting out, Keep It Simple

Developing a business plan can be very simple. A business plan is a document setting out a business's future objectives and strategies for achieving them. Your business plan can often be summarized in a short document called an executive summary:

A quick executive summary can be developed once you determine how you will operate your business.

You can simply state:

I will develop a business which buys and sells property in the Philadelphia area.

Then as you plan this out you will need to become a little more specific, because in Philly, there is Kensington square, there is West Philly, there is Germantown and so on, you get my drift, you have to get to know your target market in this process and began to cultivate relationships within that market. Do not allow yourself to become the jack of all cities and neighbor-hoods, because then you can easily become the master of none.

Some people like row homes, others like mid century moderns and contemporaries. In California we have bungalows and tract homes as well.

The craziest thing about it here in CA is that you can buy a tract home in Riverside for $300k and the same thing goes for $800k in Orange County, or you can buy a bungalow in Long Beach for $500k or the same home in Venice beach for $1.5 million. You must know your market and work within your budget.

Don't expect to shoot and eat the white unicorn, just kill and eat the Deer..

Meaning just because you have watched the million dollar flip show does not mean that you should start your flipping career at that level.

I personally went that direction around the fifth home I bought and paid for it dearly. That was the House I bought from a stripper in Vegas. She did not move out after we closed and it cost a whole lot of money and time to get an eviction completed.

There are always factors that you do not factor in at the onset that can come and eat up your potential profits, so slow and low is better than hard and fast until you have the actual capacity to handle the increased risk of taking on the properties with the bigger numbers.

After you have determined your target market, you should consider the players that are already in your space. What things are they doing that you can learn from. What is going to be your unique selling proposition that you bring to the market. How will you grow your business? How will it be financed and what do you project as a growth pattern and how will you achieve this.

Planning for Growth in your Business

Once you have your business strategy in place and you are

looking to grow your business, you will need to develop a structure for your business so that it will be considered fundable. In order to raise capital, you will need a few things in place, a proven track record, a good story, and a formal business plan.

A formal business plan is more in depth than a one page executive summary.

A table of contents for a formal business plan can include some of the following headings:

EXECUTIVE SUMMARY

MISSION & VISION

PRODUCT & SERVICE DESCRIPTION

INDUSTRY ANALYSIS

COMPETITIVE ANALYSIS

MARKET ANALYSIS

SALES & MARKETING PLAN

OPERATIONS PLAN

MANAGEMENT TEAM

FINANCIAL PLAN

• Funding Request & Terms of Investment

• Exit Strategy

This may seem like a great deal of information, and it truly is. Tip in every city there is a small business development center that provides business services and free trainings. They even have resources for business planning and free websites as well as sources for funding of small businesses. Check out an SBDC if you need help developing your business plan.

Developing your Dream Team

After you have written a business plan then you want to begin to seek and develop your team. Your team should be professionals that can cover each different aspect of your business. Trying to manage every aspect of flipping multiple

properties can become a nightmare without the help of trusted team. It is highly recommended that you start building a professional house flipping team as soon as possible. This team will help you to find, fix and sell the property – and the collective wisdom and expertise will surely help you reach your house flipping goals that much faster. You simply will not be able to do everything on your own, so enlisting your own dream team will help you be more productive and work through the eventual problems that will arise far more easily.

Your team can be comprised of real estate brokers, contractors, architects, insurance specialists, accountants and money lenders. All these specialized real estate resources can help you shorten your learning curve and get you making money flipping houses faster than you would have on your own.

The difference between a successful real estate investor and an unsuccessful one is the team he surrounds himself with.

A real estate investor is only as good as his CPA, attorney, real estate agent, inspectors, contractors, title company, etc. When it comes to pulling off all the other rules I listed, you need a strong team to be successful; if you don't have that strong team, you can bet your competition does.

A weak team will cost you time, money and headaches that you can't afford. All it takes is for your agent to negotiate poorly, your attorney to miss a contract loophole, your inspec-

tor to miss a structural problem or your contractor to screw up

to turn a profitable flip into a big loser. A couple of those can

quickly end an otherwise successful real estate career.

Once you have assessed your cash, developed an interim

business plan and identified a target market; you can then be-

gin to interview potential stakeholders or Team members for

your business.

Your first few partners for your business should be a good

quality contractor, a lender, a deal finder and an escrow per-

son.

It is extremely important for you to get your rehab numbers right at the onset of each investment for your business as well as have a contractor who will work with you in an ethical manner.

Side Note: when rehabbing and you find out that more needs to be done for the house in order to complete the rehab. This can result in a Change Order from the contractor. Change Orders are often ways for unscrupulous contractors to extract profit from an investor, under the guise of additional work needed, that was not anticipated under the original scope of work. Change Orders can eat into your profit margin.

Chapter Five

The Virtues of Partnership

Developing good partnerships can catapult you forward in your business.

Virtue #1

Split the Risk

In a partnership you get to Split the Risk: As with any investment, real estate investing carries risks and some people are unwilling to take that risk on their own. However, having a partner splits the risk (and the profits), making real estate investing an acceptable business. One way that partners begin to move forward in purchasing properties much faster is by pooling resources.

Starting any business can take a lot of resources, often too many for one person to handle themselves. If you find a person with similar interests, goals and work ethic, it may be possible to pool your resources to get off to a smooth start. Teaming up will provide expanded contacts, knowledge, cash, and money partnerships, it may also make bank financing possible, where individually you were unable to qualify during this time of strict underwriting requirements.

Partnering can also help you to overcome analysis paralysis. One thing that has hindered more potentially successful real estate investors is this one term, analysis paralysis. Have you ever found a deal and decided that you would investigate it to the point that you talked yourself out of the deal? You ever spent so much time analyzing a deal and failed to make an offer in time and lost it to another investor?

Don't get me wrong; it is vitally important to master the art of deal analysis. For someone just starting in real estate investing, **analyzing a property** can be quite an undertaking. There are hundreds of considerations when searching for that first real estate deal, so having someone else check your analysis greatly increases your odds of an accurate analysis. I can recall several properties I concluded were grand slams, only to have my business partner point out a flaw or two that I did not consider, saving us from a potentially disastrous deal. If at all possible do not buy a home by a freeway..

(Word to the Wise)

Virtue #2

Find Complementary Qualities:

Every person brings different strengths and weaknesses to a partnership. While one person may be a numbers person, the others might be able to visualize improvements to a property.

Understand what each person is good at and put those skills to use to improve your business. In my business, my partner is a great negotiator and gets a rise out of finding and getting the deal under contract, a skill I have not yet mastered. However, I am able to crunch the numbers in ways that will let us quickly know how we can purchase it and if it is ultimately going to be a great deal. Our understanding of one another allows us to leverage these skills and yield to one another when necessary.

Virtue #3

Task Division:

Real Estate Investing is challenging!

There are a lot of tasks that can easily overtake your life if you let them. Effectively and fairly dividing tasks can ensure that all partners are able to contribute to the business while not being overwhelmed.

For example, I handle day-to-day operations and make sure our web content was continuously improving. It is critical that you manage contractors and ensure our renovations remained on schedule and on budget. To contribute, my partners had to step up in other areas, like making sure our bookkeeping was up to date; and finding new deals. It may be impossible to split tasks 50/50 at all times, but as long as communication channels remain open and goals stay aligned major conflicts can be avoided.

Virtue #4

Expand your Networking:

The importance of networking cannot be overstated and networking becomes much easier when you have more than one person spreading the word. Additionally, each partner already knows people who could end up playing a part in your business, either as team members, lenders, contractors, or clients.

Accountability Partners:

People who are on a workout plan or diet often have accountability buddies to make sure they stay on track. It is human nature to slack off when things get difficult or life gets

busy, but business partners help keep each other focused. During our partnership we have faced, major illness, a marriage, many homes purchases and other life milestones.

In a one member business it would be very easy to let life slow you down, focusing on more important things with the intention of returning to investing when things slow down. However, having a business partner you do not want to disappoint keeps the business on course.

Virtue #5

Confidence/Motivation:

Beginning in real estate investing can be quite scary, especially for someone who has little experience in entrepreneurship or business. Having somebody to talk to who is feeling the same way is both calming and motivating. When obstacles arise, it is natural to doubt oneself and wonder if your pursuit of real estate investing is the right thing for you both personally and professionally, but having a partner to re- assure you can be revitalizing and motivating.

Real Estate Partnership Tips:

Virtue #6

Implement Greed Control.

Because Greed Kills:

Greed has destroyed more relationships in this business than bad marketing campaigns.

In your partnership always have written agreements. Adhere to the agreements that are set forth and be fair with your partners. A little integrity goes a long way toward longevity in this industry. There are many people who have taken the fast buck over the long term relationship and found themselves without allies when they really needed them.

Don't let little things affect your business:

Like any relationship there will be disagreements and there must be compromises. If you are the type of person who must have your way in every situation, you should probably go into business by yourself, because that is not the kind of partner most people want. Be your partners conscience from time to time, there will be opportunities that will arrive that will sound too good to be true, or the numbers just don't settle as you are analyzing the deals, don't work against your first thought about an investment. Be a partner and make decisions together. Buying an Investment property is like a marriage, when you sign on that line you now own it. The only way out is to divorce (sale) the house, it will cost you until that takes place. I mean don't buy the ugly house that you can't make pretty and still make money.

Any house can be fixed up, but at what cost..... Can you really afford to take that risk?

Virtue#7

Communicate Daily:

Seriously, talk every single day when possible. A lot can happen in a single day and both parties need to be aware of what is occurring with the other partner. When communication breaks down in a partnership it leaves much room for internal tension. If one partner is on extended vacations while the other partner is grinding away flipping houses, there is potential for the working partner to feel like he is now employed by the business and not in an evenly distributed partnership any longer. Discussing daily events and future goals keep the relationship growing and validates the reason you teamed up to begin with.

Virtue #8

Plan Ahead:

Do not start a partnership in the wrong way. Make sure the arrangement is well planned and includes an operating agreement to detail the roles and responsibilities, capital contributions, and profit splits. It should also include those things you likely do not want to talk about like what happens

when the partnership ends (either by choice or death). While partnerships have a lot of benefits, they are not for everyone, and many people are not good business partners. If you decide you would like to pursue a business partnership make one hundred percent certain you choose a business partner that will treat you fairly and has goals similar to yours.

Carefully plan the arrangement and constantly communicate. If both partners remain committed to the business, you will likely develop one that is prosperous for all parties involved.

Chapter Six

FINDING THAT FIRST FLIP

A Flipper is one who buys an asset for hopes of future income.

So your mind is now made up, you want to begin your flipping business, you have gone through all the steps and listened to the motivational tapes, read the material, signed up for the newsletter now it is time for the rubber to meet the road.. Where do you start.

You have to find your first property to flip. This is where a lot of people stop. They begin to look at websites and drive around neighborhoods and write down addresses of ugly houses but do not know what to do next. This is where many get stuck. They look

at the house to understand the house, then they hear the words from their peers who don't even know the business. After which they are faced with an internal conflict of what do I do next.. How do I even write an offer. What if the seller accepts the offer then I have to RISK MY MONEY. At this point in your development, Analysis paralysis can kick in and stop your movement into your business. I analyzed my first deal until I found myself paralyzed.

Paralyzed by the fear of the unknown.

Find a property in a geographic area you have fully researched. You should be able to buy a house for a low price, rehab it quickly and cheaply, then sell it at a higher price...and obviously make a profit.

Your real estate agent can assist you in finding houses that may not need expensive repairs unless the repairs will increase the equity. Ensure that once you do purchase the house you personally supervise the repairs and make sure they are being carried out properly and on budget. Your profit depends on the cost of the total house, including the repairs.

Taking your eye off the ball when doing the rehab is the quickest way to make your profits go up in smoke. You may find that many contractors do not have your best interest at heart. Learn about this business, learn the codes as you go along to able to be recognize what is sound and what is Mickey mouse.. When I mention Mickey mouse I mean work that is shoddy and not up to code at best. The last thing you ever want to happen is for a seller to come back to you after you have sold them the house and begin with a laundry list of things that were done wrong in the rehab process.

SPEED EQUALS PROFIT

Time is of the essence. Speed does not kill when flipping a house ...it is one of the biggest factors that will lead to profit.

The shorter the time you hold onto your investors money, the better your profits will be. So make your improvements fast.

Do the job well, but do it fast.

Stay on your contractors using these design rules

in order to do the job on budget and on time.

A fast sale in a rapidly appreciating market means more

profit for you. Even in slower markets, the same holds true.

When doing your house flipping analysis, simply determine the

potential selling price after calculating the cost of the house

and repairs, plus your monthly carrying costs of borrowing the

money needed to fund the house flip to determine your profit.

Timing is important when flipping houses – the faster you

sell, the more you make. So manage the property yourself and

implore everyone involved to work quickly because profits are

on the line.

When you flip homes, you must move quickly. Not only do

you need to buy quickly, you need to sell the house fast -- and

that means you must sell under-market.

If you wait for the buyer who is willing to pay top dollar,

you'll wait- a long time and increase your risk that the market may turn against you. You'll also lose valuable time that could be used flipping other homes.

If your profit is $30,000 per deal and you flip three houses in a year, you pocket a sweet $90,000. But let's say you hold out for more profits and you can only turn two houses in a year. Even though your profit might be $40,000 a deal, you still earn $10,000 less. Got it?

If you consider the implications, you'll see that in order to sell a home under-market and still make a profit, the key is to buy it inexpensively.

That often means it's a good idea to buy property that has been foreclosed on. You have to master your market and find good Realtors to work with.

Set your Goals

In the real estate business, a fixer-upper can be a smart way to get started in the business and earn good money at the same time. Buying and selling fixer-uppers, when done with discretion and with good buying judgment, can prove to be a good way to earn money without having to invest heavily – especially when done right.

When starting out in a fixer-upper business, you will first have to consider many things. After learning what you can, then proceed to drawing realistic expectations and plans to put your business into action. From here, you can then set goals and work on plans to meet those goals. While the fixer upper business offers attractive, high-income ventures, if not done properly, can drive one into serious debt if not done properly.

For those unacquainted with the term, fixer upper homes are real estate bought from distressed homeowners, fixed up (hence the term fixer) and sold at market prices. The sellers can be one of many types. We have purchased fixers from probate sales, short sales, standard sales, bank sales, auctions, tax liens sales, private parties, on market off market, in state and out of state. In a way it is like finding a diamond in the rough, breaking it down, polishing it, and sending it back to the market for a great price.

Many have gone on to be millionaires from this kind of venture. If you look at it, theoretically, it makes a lot of sense.

However, no matter how attractive it may seem to be, this type of business isn't without its risks.

Fix and Flips involve a lot of money, assumptions and risks. You assume that the real estate you are buying can be fixed up and sold at a higher price. You also assume that the house can be brought up to a state where it is attractive to those seeking a home to move into.

If you put all these intangibles together, you will find that the risk may be a little too high for some people. In fact, this is the reason that these ventures are high-profit ones, they are also high risk.

You can, however, reduce this risk by doing good background studies, setting realistic goals, drawing up good plans, and making calculated risks. Here are some good tips on building a good fixer upper business venture.

1. Goals – You will have to set realistic goals for your business. Fixer upper homes can earn a good deal of money, but it wouldn't hurt to set a conservative figure as you learn the ropes. Sometimes conservative is good – especially when you are just starting to get the hang of a venture. Some people set unrealistic goals, like aiming for $100,000,000 at the onset, hoping against all hope they can make and sell at an incredible rate. However, it would be better to keep with a realistic figure. Most investors will agree that $100,000 is a good amount to expect per year in a fixer upper venture.

This figure is taken by considering the sale of 5 fixed up houses with a cut of $20,000 per house. This isn't a bad figure to start with. And you will be able to adjust better figures as you learn more about the business.

You will also have to consider what this business will mean to your financial system, can you give up your day job just to focus on this business? Will you do this on your own free time? Or will you try a little of both to see where you do best?

What to know before you flip

While the investors above have each employed their own strategies, and often met with success, home flipping is a risky business dependent on rising real estate prices and low mortgage rates. In short, it's not as easy as it looks.

Investors must also be careful of the tax consequences in their quest for a quick buck. If you sell a property in less than a year, which most investors do, profits are taxed as short-term capital gains, which are taxed at the same rates as regular income. (If you were to hold on to the property for a year or more, you would typically be taxed at a lower rate on those capital gains.) Plus, the Internal Revenue Service may consider you a real estate dealer, instead of an investor, if you are successful enough at flipping. That means your profits would be taxed at the same rates as ordinary income *and* you'll have to pay Social Security and Medicare taxes on those earnings.

So before you start your investment business — or decide to buy even one investment property — make sure you have an adequate emergency fund and are maxing out your retirement account. It will make things easier if the red-hot real estate market starts to chill.

Property Type and Exit Strategy

1. Properties – Make sure you don't put all your eggs in one basket. This could lead you to losing more than you are willing to in one venture. Depending on your source of financing, you could handle one or more properties at a time. Again, it will be advisable to start slowly before gradually increasing the number of properties you handle at one time.

2. Sell or Keep – Some investors will decide to fix and keep, instead of fix and sell. If, with your research, you learn that you stand to earn more if you hold the property for a while, then do so.

3. If you see that you don't stand to earn a lot by keeping it, then put it on the market as soon as you see fit. On the other

hand, if you notice that prime property is coming towards the property you are fixing up, holding on for a while can possibly yield you a better return in the future.

4. There are many different types of properties that can be purchased to be resold for a profit. Single Family and 1-4 Unit Dwellings are the most prevalent in our cities, and also can be purchased for smaller amounts of money. There are also commercial, multifamily, Industrial, Specialty and Land trans-actions that all can make an investor good returns; however in order to work these more complicated property types, you would need to develop additional skills and obtain specialized knowledge in order to build a competitive business that would focus on those property types.

Chapter Seven

Flipping Mastery

In order to grow and scale your business and become a full time investor, there are a few key skills that you will need to learn. You should know more than the average person who has watched HGTV, you have won more than you lost and you are ready to say goodbye to the 9 to 5 job. It is in this place in which it becomes absolutely necessary that we consider mastering our business. In order to become an expert at your chosen profession, you must possess the knowledge needed to set plans in motion and have an understanding about the ins and outs of the business. I will go through a few key fundamentals in this chapter that I hope will help you to understand what it takes to build a house flipping business.

Fundamental #1

Master your Market

In this business you will learn to calculate your potential profit when you buy the house. Before you consider purchasing any property you will need to know what the maximum amount that you can pay for the property is. This is your Max Allowable Offer. Or MAO. Your MAO considers many factors and is padded to reflect a reasonable profit that you will earn when you resell the asset.

KEY Thought: You make your money when you buy.

In order to calculate a Max Allowable Offer you would need to consider the following data points.

1. After Repaired Value
2. Financing Costs
3. Resale Costs
4. Monthly Payment Amount
5. Average days on market (Resale)
6. Length of Rehab Process.

7. Rehab Amount

Market Metrics

Purchasing for Appreciation

We create value in property by forcing appreciation into an asset through the process of rehabilitation and renovation.

Fundamentally the dollars you invest in a property and dollars that are returned with interest.

Finding property in a good market is key, however you can make money in an appreciating market or a market that is flat or down, if you know and use the fundamentals. You should also have multiple exit strategies and an understanding of which strategy to apply in order to have a successful nimble investment business.

You want to always flip property in an appreciating market. If you live in an area that isn't appreciating, you might be better off flipping somewhere else. If you are still looking to buy in a market that is flat, you should be looking for cash flow proper-ties or value add deals in order to create the equity that you need in order for the investment to be profitable.

And if home prices are dropping, you are playing Russian roulette by getting into this game no matter where you are. Just the same, you can't predict when the market is going to turn.

To be on the safe side, make sure that you'll be able to hold on to the home as a rental property for a while, if need be. In order to understand the market you are buying in you can do the following:

1. Call the top three realtors in the area. These are people that you can track that have closed a considerable vol-ume of homes. You want to ask them about the neigh-borhood and homes that they have sold in the area. Also ask them how they think the market is doing in that area. Is it trending up or slowing down. You will find that between three top producing people there will be simi-

larities and differences in what they report back to you.

2. You can also review the local real estate market analysis and heat maps that are provided online in order to get another viewpoint. Websites like Trulia have an area which provides analysis of the local markets. The data points are average home price, avg price per square foot and median rent that are being paid in the area.

3. You can also look at walk scores and crime stats in order to get a viewpoint of the amount of crime that occurs in the area that you are looking to purchase in because this will be a big factor in pricing your property when you attempt to resell the asset.

4. Walk the property, drive the comparable properties and get a feel for the neighborhood.

Fundamental #2

Learn to Manage your Financial Risk

Due Diligence Practices

One vital skill that real estate investors must learn in order to be successful in this industry is risk management. Risk management is more commonly called due diligence. Due diligence is the standard methodology of assessing and mitigating risk. Developing and Implementing a regular due diligence process must become an integral part of your acquisitions process as well as asset management practices for your current holdings.

Our aim is to minimize the problems you buy, so that you can properly manage Financial Risk.

Any property that you purchase will have unknown risks associated. There could be leaking pipes, hidden mold, rats in the attic, or even water intrusion; there are many things that can happen to a house, and it becomes your responsibility once you become the new owner of the property. You may be buying problems that you don't know about.

Some of the things to consider when buying are the following.

Double check and verify the Property Condition

You may want to have a number of third party agencies involved in the acquisition process for your business. Depending upon what type of property you are looking to purchase this list of professionals may change from time to time. Water intrusion specialist, Property inspector, Contractor, Chimney inspector, Mold Inspector, Sewer Inspector, Electrician, Plumber, Soil Engineer, Foundation Inspector, Surveyor, Architect, Mechanical Engineer. All of these specialties are vital at different times in your business. Reach out and meet a number of them in your marketplace or ask people you trust for referrals of who they would recommend.

Check existing City Permits:

I bought a nightmare in the desert.

A beautiful home with great views and amenities, along with an illegal room addition. Everything looked normal and I had all of my professionals walk through the home, we looked at all of the visible traits and characteristics of the home. But the part that we could not see cost us thousands of dollars to find and fix.

There were three main problems in this house,

1. The property had an addition that was installed without a foundation for the enclosed wall.

2. The property had spliced electrical circuits inside the walls which were installed with extension cords which created a high risk of fire.

3. There were no permits for an enclosed patio on file with

the city.

The home was actually a firetrap with no foundation on the rear.. Go figure.

I can not stress the fact enough that it is better to know what structures are legal with the city before you conclude your purchase. Take the time out and go to the city and pull all existing permits on the property that you are going to buy. There are also web based services in larger service areas that provide information on code violations like Zimas in Los Angeles or the city department of building and safety which tracks the permits and violations that have been logged against each property. Sellers do not always disclose material facts regarding distressed property.

You must perform your due diligence, you cannot always rely on your project manager or contractor to get it right the first time, so before you close I recommend seeing the property physically, and traveling to the city your self. Ask about set-backs and how much of the existing structure that are legal. Find out if the property is on city sewage or septic tank. A septic tank can kill your whole investment. Closing on the property without knowing can cause you to have wasted investment capital without the planned ability to execute and successfully sell the asset.

When you are purchasing multifamily project, always check to see if you have a master meter. You may be responsible for utilities for the tenants and the cost of water, trash and gas will be a monthly expense that needs to be factored into the analysis; so that you can know if you can afford this new venture or if it is dead in the water.

This Business is not for the overly lax and definitely not for the lazy.

You can hire good people on your team but ultimately **the buck comes from you.**

When you perform due diligence it is for your own protec-

tion and the protection of your investors and partners.

Mismanaged Risk, can be very costly when investing in real estate.

KEY Risk Management Principle #3

Always run the numbers:

They say in business culture numbers don't lie. My method for flipping houses comes down to a formula spelled out on a spreadsheet. Finding an excel based spreadsheet that you can understand is very important. You can also use certain apps that are available in the marketplace to help you to run the initial numbers on properties that you are analyzing. When you are considering a new purchase you analysis will take into account a number of factors which will help to inform your viewpoint of the property from an investors point of view.

Your analysis should answer the questions listed below.

1. Is this property located in a neighborhood that is desir-

able to others and likely to sell quickly

2. How much is the asking price.

3. How much is the rehabilitation for the asset.

4. How much are comparable properties selling for in the area.

5. What type of finish products are other investors using in the area to get top dollar.

6. How much can I leverage from a bank or private lender.

7. How much will the loan cost.

8. I need to include both points, fees, and interest that will be paid.

9. How much is my down payment.

10. How long will I own this investment property before I can execute on an exit.

11. What is the average days on the market for other properties that have sold in the neighborhood.

12. How much would the property rent for if I was unable to sell it in a shifting or down market?

13. What is maximum allowable offer price for this property based upon the factors listed above.

On the current home I hope to sell, I plan to spend no more than $40,000 on repairs and expect a return on investment of about 16 percent based on my selling price.

When you're doing these deals, it's not about falling in love with the kitchen — it's a math problem, If the numbers work, it seems less risky.

The formula has worked out so far, even with such a high expected rate of return.

We just did a flip on a Triplex we bought that was owned by a bank for $240,000 with $5000 down and $40,000 in improvements. We sold it for $389,000. After paying back the mortgage for the apartments, we made $69,000 on the sale, which is a 35 percent return on our $45,000 investment.

What's changed from the last housing boom is that most flip-pers are now unable to buy homes with 0 percent down.

Banks will not finance a deal without 25 percent down, so cre-ative strategies and good relationships with private money lenders are key to your business success in this market.

We plan to stick to the formula, using the earnings from one deal to fund the next. Or we will use equity creation strategies to raise the money needed to buy the next set of homes.

Never forget that you make your money when you buy, you can make a nice profit in a short period of time. Buying homes today can be a very expensive undertaking. Nevertheless, it can also bring highly valuable and profitable assets

With the growing market value of most homes, some home special-ists say that people should think about their lending before they even think about buying their homes. In this way, you can estimate and foresee what kind of home you can afford. If you are looking to become an investor this is not the time to get wrapped up in the emotion of buying and hoping for the dream home. It is wise to stand back at this point and begin to look at the home for what it is, a means to an end.

The home is a commodity, the lenders who will lend you the money at prime plus one or 12% are not looking at the home with any concern for the amenities, they are simply looking at the yield of their investment in your business. The home has no place in your heart, it has its best use in your portfolio building your asset pool. It has a place in your overall financial plan of how you are going to accomplish specific financial goals with the acquisition and hold or sale of the asset.

This is an area that many potential investors get stuck, the emotion of the buy, not the logic of the investment. So you muster up enough guts to talk to your local banker.

You walk into one of the big four and say I want to buy an investment property they will sit you down and run through the whole scenario with you to bring you to their reality and assessment of you and your buying ability. What they don't know is that there are ways to buy real estate which actually require no credit, no cash out of pocket, no cash reserves to be shown etc. so going to your major bank should not be your ultimate destination or end all for your to assess your ability to become an investor.

For this reason, buying homes that are below the market value is sensible. You may not be aware of it but it is possible that you can buy your investment home below market value.

Yet, it doesn't necessarily mean that buying a home below market value is the only way to make a wise investment in to-day's economic environment.

Buying homes below market value requires guts, strength of mind, and patience to get the best deal. Keep in mind that there is a very strong reason why these kinds of houses are being sold below market value. And most often than not, these reasons aren't things that are readily disclosed by the sellers of the properties. I have found that many sellers of distressed properties never get inspections done that reveal the true nature of the condition of the property therefore your job required due diligence in order for you to make an informed decision on whether to buy a property that you are interested in. There are many reports that are normally ordered and some that are specific to the deal and we will discuss these further in the due diligence practices portion of this book.

Buying a fix and flip home is one of the best targets if you really want to buy a home below market value. These kinds of dwellings are usually being sold on the market at lower prices because of their structural and cosmetic defects.

Fix and flip homes are a great strategy to pursue and should be in part of your portfolio. In fact, you can fix them up and they will be as comfortable as the others, but you have to consider the cost of expenses you have to take on when fixing a home.

However, there are other factors that you have to keep in mind before deciding on buying a fix and Flip home. Here are some of the factors you have to consider as well:

Buying homes below market value like fix and flip homes may not be good enough if the market condition is at its worst.

This means that if you plan to make a profit out of the present value of your fixer home and suddenly the market condition has turned bitter, the idea of buying homes below market value may not sound like the best methodology.

Keep in mind that home market values are constantly fluctuating in value. If this is the case, buying homes below market value such as fix and flip homes may bring you increased risk of loss if you have not done proper due diligence on the asset, neighborhood, and macro market factors before the acquisition is complete.

Fundamental Three

Understand how to Rehab:

In order to make money in this business, you must understand what work a house really needs, what that's going to cost and how that will impact your offer. That sets the stage for you to do all the work, sell the house under-market and still make a profit.

Your best bet is to buy real estate that needs cosmetic work that is inexpensive to perform yet makes the property much more attractive to buyers. You can't always rely on the Contractor to perform at levels that make you money. You can always expect that the contractor will consider his bottom line first, as he is also in business to make a profit. This can mean two things to you, the contractor will charge you on material and labor or if you do not have a full scope set in your contract and pay him per day, he may work more slowly to drag time out if you have not had a set budget in place for the renovation of the property.

One of the the problems that I have experienced is that the scope of work changes as you get deeper into the renovation of the property. Case in point, it is always nice to have great ideas as an investor to update the layout of older properties to the lifestyles of today, however if you open a wall; you now own it.

Whatever is in it, is now your responsibility to bring up to current building standards. This may cause you to have to rewire a whole property because your contractor opened a wall and you came to see that the existing electrical is substandard as compared to the current building practices.

That additional work is vital for your resale, costs you more money than you had budgeted and your contractor will gladly do the work. But how much more is it really going to cost you now.. One thing to consider when facing this type of challenge is that if you pay it out now, you are more likely to be able to recover it later on a faster, easier more profitable resale. End user buyers are typically not visionaries like the investor. They

can not see that the old electrical in one portion of the house is not an issue because it was placed under past codes, all they can see is what they heard in the media about buyer beware and they will run not walk from your house which is now half way done to one that has been fully upgraded.

Therefore, In the beginning of your career it is wise to decline or wholesale any projects that need major structural repair. Hire a good contractor, and get him to inspect the property. Don't buy homes that need bathroom or kitchen renovation unless you are ready to take on that level of renovation. That type of work will cost big bucks and take lots of time. Look for a simple deal when you are simply starting out.

KEY Principle: The key to making money flipping houses is to buy for the right price and cut down your risk.

You buy right when you understand your market and your repair plan. You cut risk by using cash, creating credit, minimizing borrowed money and by completing the flip fast.

If you are interested in getting into this business, your next step is to figure out how much money you have or can put your hands on active investors. You may consider borrowing.

Next, scope out the market that makes the most sense and find good Realtors to work with. Take these steps first and then make sure you expertly understand the market and property rehab. At that point, you're ready to go.

Chapter Eight

Wholesaling to build your Savings.

I learned to wholesale properties after I had already learned to flip properties. In real estate transactions, it is He who is in control that really matters. Control can give you the privileges of ownership.

Control gives you some of the privileges of Ownership

10 ways to take control of an investment property.

1. Sales Contract
2. Trust Agreements
3. Joint Venture Contracts
4. Equity Play Mezzanine Lending
5. Notes And Trust Deeds
6. Subject to Existing Financing Purchasing
7. Lease with an option

8. Option Agreement

9. Assuming the Loans

10. Land Contract

11. Probate Award

12. Inheritance and more

A wholesaler is a person who takes control of another person's property through the use of a sales contract. People sometimes wholesale for a period of time and switch business strategies after they have increased their cash position and moved into the method of buying the property to flip. Wholesalers sell their access to the paper which controls the sale of the property. They trade their negotiated position to a cash investor who then purchases the property for the terms set, and proceed to fix up and resell the asset. It is not uncommon to earn over 6 figures using this strategy in our marketplace, honestly it is much easier than flipping but there are many aspects that must be in place in order for this strategy to be profitable for your business.

A wholesaler is a real estate sales contract middleman. Rather than actually selling or buying the property, they put it under contract with contingencies specific clause within a contract, until they can find a buyer to complete the sale. A wholesaler gets paid by doing all the legwork of finding a buyer for the seller's property. He essentially makes money by selling his rights to purchase the home within the sales contract.

However, just because you don't need a license to be a wholesaler does not mean that wholesaling can be done as a hobby or a job on the side. While people can be landlords or flip houses along with having full-time careers outside of the real estate business, wholesaling is a lot more like a full-time job. Wholesalers need to constantly be out on the road, looking for new properties, working and expanding their network, and staying up to date on all the real estate industry news and trends.

How does wholesaling work?

As previously stated, wholesalers use contingencies to put a property under contract without purchasing the property directly themselves. You have probably heard of contingencies even if you have never heard of wholesaling as they have become a part of every real estate contract in recent years.

The more contingencies in the contract, the less likely the offer will be accepted.

Contingencies are clauses in a contract that allow one person or party to back out of a deal within a specified time period with no consequences if certain requirements are not met. There are contingencies for everything from pest inspections to making sure the buyer can sell their current home before buying a new one.

We often use an Inspection Contingency to allow at least 10 days to make sure that everything is in order. While a new wholesaler may think that placing several contingencies on a property will give them more time to find a buyer, this is not ideal in a hot market or with a quality investment property.

The more contingencies in the contract, the less likely they will be accepted. Remember that a seller does not have to accept your "offer" so you want to make it as simple and appealing as possible.

However, wholesalers can usually make a profit if they find a good enough deal. You can sell a good number of the properties you tie up as long as the home is priced right. This confidence comes from having a strong network of potential buyers, which is why building a network is so important for those just starting out.

Who is a target buyer of wholesale property?

Wholesalers usually sell their property or contracts to real estate investors, particularly those who specialize in flipping houses. The majority of the time, the properties they deal with are in need of repair. They also largely accept payment in cash, lines of credit, or hard money loans, naturally making their deals more accessible to investors than the typical home buyer.

How can you start wholesaling to build your warchest of funds?

As a wholesaler, you will need to know the sale prices of your real estate market well enough in order to identify a well-priced property. You will also need to have an understanding of real estate transactions and a network of ready buyers.

You can resell just about anything as long as it's priced right. Not all real estate markets are ideal for wholesaling. Typically, these kinds of deals are best suited to areas where there is a large

amount of under priced property or distressed housing with not enough buyers. The best wholesalers are the ones with a strong network and working knowledge of what they are selling.

In order to be the most effective you should have a working knowledge of the product you are selling. In this case if you are selling a house in Beverly Hills, it is up to you to know what questions need to be answered. What is my ARV or after repaired value, is this Beverly hills proper or post office, (each area commands its own price and has a different level of prestige.),

What is the story behind the home? Is it a standard of bank sale? What is wrong with the property, what is the repair cost needed, is it a hillside property, are there any code violations on file etc, etc.

If you can answer these types of questions quickly you are more likely to be able to procure a buyer when the buyer arrives at your door.

If you are new to wholesaling, one way to start is by joining a real estate wholesale company that specializes in these kinds of transactions. While you can wholesale on your own without being part of any organization, those without an existing network of real estate professionals may want to join one to get their feet in the investing waters first.

Chapter Nine

Finding Funding for your Business

Funding is always available for good real estate deals. If you learn the art of finding, rehabbing and flipping a good deal, other people will be willing to invest their money with you.

The truth of the matter here is that you can get other peoples money to work for you. You can earn more without placing your cash in as an investment. While it seems counter intuitive – who, in his right mind, would ever hope to get good returns on investments when he or she hasn't put in any investments at all, one must think – it truly is possible to get other people's money, time, and expertise to work for your own benefit.

OPM Other People's Money

One way to think of OPM (Other People's Money) working for your benefit is to think of how most people expect to make earnings from fix and flip ventures.

First off, most people would want to purchase the property it-self. They could do this in a couple of different ways. They could purchase the homes out of their savings or take out loans to pay for the property.

This method, while good in itself, has some limitations. If you use your savings to buy property for a venture – and for some unforeseen reason, the venture goes bust and you are unable to sell the property, then you may have practically thrown your life savings out the window.

You can make other people's money work for you here. For example, what if you take a 95% seller's financing plan. This means you only pay for around 5% of the property's value. Then, you proceed to lease the house to tenants. The money you make from the rentals can be used to pay for the loan.

In the end, theoretically speaking, you would have only paid 5% cold cash for the property, and made the property itself – with the help of its tenants – pay for the property the rest of the way. If the property costs $100,000, then that means you only pay $5,000 to own the property after some time – with extra income to boot. Not a bad proposition now, is it?

This is, in effect, having other people pay for something you will own in the future, and is one of the smart ways to make Investments.

You could also use other people's resources such as time and expertise when trying to make money from fixer homes.

For example, if you aren't well-versed in renovating properties, why not have other people do it, and make a profit at the same time.

How? Take for example a home that is sold by a distressed owner – house unkempt, needing repairs. Now, as an investor yourself, the first thing you would want to do is think of how you can purchase and renovate the place, and then sell it on the market.

But what if, instead, you make plans to purchase the property and then show the property to other cash buyers who may want to take the property from your hands and do the hard work of renovating and selling the property on the market.

You can then sell the property again to this partner and have them renovate and sell the property. Just don"t forget to take your profit from the pay you will be asking of them for the property! This, in technical terms, is called flipping.

If you look at it closely, you will have had made somewhere close to what most people in the same business make without even having to do the hard work required of them – remodeling, renovating, and marketing. The technique there, however, is that you will have to be aware of how to choose potentially great properties.

If you have an eye for that then it won't be much of a problem.

If you do this, you will have effectively used other people's expertise and time in helping you make a good profit. This is a great way to leverage other"s assets to work for your advantage.

Where Do You Get the Money for Fix and Flips?

For most people, seeking financing for fixer ventures will prove to be one of the more challenging things to consider.

Some of those that have been able to save up might consider investing their savings into such a venture.

However, this would be tantamount to putting all your eggs in one basket. If you lose the basket, there goes your future.

And that would be financial suicide, by any measure. If you are looking for good financing for your fix and flip, here are a few good alternatives.

Regular Bank Loans

1. Housing Loans – The US Department of Housing and Urban Development 203 (k) rehabilitation mortgages is one of the best solutions if you are looking for a single, low-interest solution to purchasing and fixing up a home property with one loan. This is a great alternative to taking out multiple higher interest loans that could cripple your finances – you can instead have just one loan that is decidedly easier to pay off.

While this is a great alternative to other loans and mortgages, it does have guidelines. For one, it is subject to guidelines submitted by the Federal Housing Administration – these guidelines may also vary from state to state.

For example in order to be eligible for this loan, it has to have improvement costs of at least $5000 for a one to four condominium or family residence unit. After eligibility, the loan then becomes available with wonderfully low interest rates for terms as long as 30 years!

And to top this, you will only have to pay about 3 percent down payment if you are an owner occupier, and 15 percent if you are an investor. It is also available is you want to finance the repair not only of properties you don't own yet, but properties that are already in your fold as well.

If you want a nice, low-interest, long-term or short-term financing, you will have to be an attractive client to most banks.

For you to fall under the attractive client bracket, you will have to have your financial house in order.

If you have a bad credit history – having debts left and right and defaulting on previous loans, then you will probably have trouble getting good loans. For such dire situations, the only opportunities that present themselves at this point will be high-interest loans.

While some people will be glad to have someone offer a loan at this rate, you should always remember that every percent counts. And that every percent could very well spell a few more hundred or even thousands of dollars in payments yearly. You, in the eyes of lenders, will have become a high-risk client, which warrants the increase in interest you will be experiencing.

The best way to get attractive loans is to get your financial house in order before setting out for available financing. Without such measures, you will end up with financing that maybe too hard to handle.

In a nutshell, the best way to get into the good graces of the lenders is to pay off existing debts (or to at least settle with previous lenders for a payment plan), and to avoid getting into new debt immediately.

There are many forms of financing available, each with its own idiosyncrasies. Study all the terms of these loans before entering into them and learn how each one fits your current financial situation before considering any one of them.

2. Other Sources of Capital – You could also use any number of private lenders available to you. Private mortgages or second mortgages are common among those that purchase Fix and Flips.

Private money loans are loans that are made for business purposes by individuals or lending agencies that are in the marketplace that provide capital for real estate investors. They have multiple loan programs especially designed for real estate investors that often have underwriting criteria that are more relaxed than major banks. More recently there has been the influx of capital providers that are more aggressive and will even provide all the money that is needed in order to purchase the property.

3. Some also pay visits to their banks for loans. There are many portfolio products that are available to consumers directly from banker. Did you know that while the mortgage meltdown happened, there were banks that were still providing

loans with no documentation required to certain bank customers. In Los Angeles there is Cathay Bank who maintains a portfolio product which will provide funding for purchases with stated income.

4. In the mortgage marketplace today there are many non prime loan products which were developed by Impacc mortgage corporation that will provide much needed purchase and refinance loans for investors and entrepreneurs alike. You can expect for non qualified mortgage products which are not subject to the Consumer Financial Protection Bureau's, TILA-RESPA Integrated Disclosure (TRID) rules, to be a resource for borrowers that need to use alternative forms of documentation for income and assets. The programs include features like:

   a. Asset Depletion
   b. Bank Statement programs for both W2 wage earners and Business owners.
   c. Stated Income and Verified Assets
   d. Expanded Debt to income ratios
   e. Loans that will allow the property to qualify based upon

its income, not the income of the borrower.

f.   Investment property loans for borrowers without a Social Security Number.

g. Investment property loans for professional Real Estate
Investors.

h. Investment property loans to Corporate Entities, ie.
Corporation, LLC, LLP and Trusts.

5. Joint Venture Partners.

Joint Venture Partners, also known as JV Equity Partners, are
available in the real estate investment marketplace. A seasoned real estate investor can scale their business by working
with JV Partners. A JV Partner will provide the equity that is
needed in order to purchase a home for the purpose of fix and
flip or holding for a longer period of time. Many JV Equity
providers are also called gap lenders. A Gap lender is a lender
who provides the capital that is needed to fill the gap in the
investment. For example, if you are purchasing a home for
$100,000 and have secured a loan that will provide $65,000,
you still have a gap of $35,000 plus costs. If the home has po-
tential to resale for a profit, you may be able to find a gap

lender who will provide the capital that is needed in order to purchase and rehab the property. The gap lender would provide the additional equity probably $30,000 and all or a portion of the additional rehab money needed to fix up and resale the property.

However their business model will require that they also receive a portion of sales proceeds as well as interest on the capital that they have deployed into the investment property. 50/50 shared profit split arrangements are common in the marketplace.

Seller Financing

One of the most powerful tools that I have found in finding distressed property has been seller financing. Any seller with equity can lend you their equity for terms while you perform the actions that are needed to make their property appreciate in value.

If you can find a seller who is willing to work with His equity in

Creative ways, you may have found a goldmine. Encouraging your seller to be his own banker is an awesome way to create alternative credit. The seller can help you as an investor create your down payment, closing costs, and other investment costs. The seller can even pay the rehabilitation cost and partner with you in order to have the rehabilitation completed on a property.

Think outside the box when negotiating with a seller.

Develop on menu and off menu items when you are thinking through your purchase scenario, because if you can create a win win for both you and your seller, you may be able to increase ROI on both sides of the transaction.

In some cases, seller financing provides a better alternative

to other loans. Property managers themselves can

finance the purchase of their own property, with you bringing in

as little as 5 percent of the total price. This method is

more amenable to people than having to pay the whole thing

out of their own pocket immediately.

In any case, you should find a financial instrument that is acceptable and payable in agreeable terms since not all available financing options are practical or useful for your purpose. You should keep a look out for low-interest, long-term loans that are available.

Of course, such attractive loans are only available on certain conditions. And to get the better deals, you will have to be able to clear underwriting criteria.

Any legally responsible way that you can obtain an investment property is a good way, please utilize this information as a guidebook to begin your real estate investing career.

In closing, I would like to say, thank you for going on the journey to financial freedom with me. There are certain abiding principles that should be used as internal guidelines for running a real estate investment business successfully.

I have been blessed to spend years developing a business acumen that has accelerated our group of companies to funding and purchasing millions in real property in a short amount of time. Please use this as a reference and research some of the methodologies to expand your working knowledge until you reach the pinnacle of your success in business.

www.ingramcontent.com/pod-product-compliance
Lightning Source LLC
Chambersburg PA
CBHW021434170526
45164CB00001B/234